Imprints In The Sand

Raja's Insights

Raja Williams

Creative Talents Unleashed

GENERAL INFORMATION

Imprints In The Sand
Raja's Insights
By
Raja Williams

1st Edition: 2015

This Publishing is protected under Copyright Law as a "Collection". All rights for all submissions are retained by the Individual Author and or Artist. No part of this publishing may be Reproduced, Transferred in any manner without the prior **WRITTEN CONSENT** of the "Material Owner" or its Representative Creative Talents Unleashed.

Creative Talents Unleashed

www.ctupublishinggroup.com

Publisher Information
1st Edition: Creative Talents Unleashed
CreativeTalentsUnleashed@aol.com

Library of Congress Control Number: 2016921556
Copyright © 2015: Raja Williams

ISBN-13: 978-0-9968292-0-5 (Creative Talents Unleashed)
ISBN-10: 0996829202

$11.95

Credits

Foreword

Tony Haynes

Dedication

I dedicate this collection of poems to my five amazing children; *Jarren, Derrick, Kevin, Keija,* and *Isiah*. You fuel my push to succeed, keep me laughing, and love BIG in your each individual way. Thank you, my journey would be incomplete without you. I love you.

Foreword

"From nowhere to now here…" Tell me how profound is this… question mark and exclamation point. It is, and it really is, yet it isn't really what you think. Though it is, it is still and instills so much more. My friend, the majestic and poetic Raja Williams' insightful *'Imprints In The Sand'* will take the reader on a journey through the wonders of introspection and perspective. The caveat remains, it will take you there and you'll actually be here, wherever here and there ever was. If this sounds deliberately confusing, I mean it to be, because the key to interpretive reading from the view of the insightful, is to rise above and glance at new heights with a mind opened to receive. With this expressed, absorb the heights and depths of Raja's gift and be moved to now here, beautifully out of nowhere.

Tony Haynes

Author, Lyricist, Song Writer

Preface

Time continues to press forward whether we are prepared for its movement or not. We leave imprints of ourselves and our life experiences on our daily walks in life. What kind of imprints are you leaving? How do you view life?

"I am nowhere"

"I am now here"

Amazing the difference space can make.

Introduction

The journey continues... I am constantly striving to live in each moment of the day, to be present. Although at times, I drift off, and get lost, I always come back and reconnect. It takes daily practice to stay grounded and remain in the present moment of now.

Pressed between these pages you will find moments of reflection, observations of life, questions I ponder, and hopefully insight's of a writers soul. Enjoy my journey, walk with me, through *Imprints In The Sand*.

Table of Contents

Dedication	v
Foreword	vii
Preface	ix
Introduction	xi

Nowhere

Nirvana	1
Mother Earths Echo	2
I Am Not My Father	4
Cruise Control	5
Losing Hope	7
Her	8
Desire	9
Now	10
Buried Alive	11
Don't Look Back	12
Worn	13

Table of Contents

Upside Down	14
The Climb	15
Living in Loves Illusion	16
Kissing the Rain	17
My Muse is Gone	18
Break Through	19
Thorns	20
Self-Image	21
Rise of the Holes	22
Walking In	23
Unconditionally	24
Forgotten	25
Some Day	26
Broken Compass	27
Finger Jams	28
I Found the Hidden Self	29
Respectfully Aging	31

Table of Contents

Now Here

Broken Heart	34
Time Keeps on Slipping Into the Future	35
I Am Love	36
The Reach	37
Soul House	38
Spiritual Fool	39
My Wish For You	40
Path to Dharma	41
Observation	42
Incomplete	43
Katana	44
Broken Mirrors	45
Shadow Effect	46
The Machine	48
Landscapes	50
All of Me	51
Ebb and Flow	52

Table of Contents

Amplified Love	53
When I see you	54
Understanding Emptiness	55
Without Notice	56
Divorce: Losing What You Know	57
Summer Rain	59
HELLO SUN, Goodbye Moon - A Mother and Son Collaboration	60
Personal Fiction	62
Q & A's with Myself	64

Epilogue

About the Author	69
Raja's Links	70

Imprints In The Sand

Raja's Insights

Raja Williams

Creative Talents Unleashed

Nowhere

Nirvana

We are living in the paradise
Of many manifestations

Because you are life
And life cannot die

You are in the trees
Living upon this land

You are the butterflies
Taking first flight

You are the fish
That swim down stream

You are in the air
That we breathe

The sun, moon
And the stars

Where ever you go
You are there . . .

Waiting for yourself.

Mother Earths Echo

Can you hear me . . .

Can you hear the whisper of a gentle breeze
The roar of the winds
The crashing of the surf onto the beach
The arrival of seawater upon your feet
The gurgle of the rivers water tumbling over rocks
The pitter-patter of rain dropping from the sky
Thunder crashing, animal calls . . .

Can you hear at all?

Our land is screaming out to us
But we are not listening
We are ignoring the cries of our suffering planet
Losing connection to Mother Nature
Brought on by Urban Sprawl

We have lost the purity of the air we breathe!
We have lost the purity of the water we need to drink!
We endanger ourselves through the food we eat!
Don't you think it's time to get in sync?

What would Mother Earth say if she could talk to me?

She would tell us . . .

Learn to listen inwardly . . .
Hear the sounds of the earth
In your very own heart beat

Imprints In The Sand

Take time to expand and learn
Connect spiritually with our land

Reach out a helping hand to those in need
Be in sync with the world

Because the world outside of you
Slowly transforms . . .
And becomes the world inside of you.

We are one, we are the world.

I Am Not My Father

As I watched him walk away,
I realized the burdens he has carried
He carries with him;
His father's sins

They are attached to his soul
And anchored into his DNA

He walks like his father
He talks like his father
His angry outbursts performed;
Just like his father

In a heated moment of anger between us
I accusingly yell out . . .
"You're just like your father,
why would you want to be like that?"

The silence cuts with a knife
His stare;
Kills me dead where I stand

That was the last time I saw him
He walked out the door;
His last words . . .

"I Am Not My Father!"

Three days later . . . He died of a drug overdose
He died;
Just like his father.

Cruise Control

Let me ask you something . . .

Are you fully living your life?

Or are you in groove with the routine
That keeps you on the grind
Turning a nickel to a dime?

From autopilot
To cruise control
Living "this" life
Paying the toll . . .

But what do I really know?

I know that I got to pay
For this shelter
The roof over my head
Exchanging time for money
The life of the dead!

Buried inside this body of mine . . .

I have a dream,
I have a life!

But damn . . .
I am stuck in the rat race of 9 to 5.

I have no time to myself
Or for anything else!
Exhausted from the mentality

Imprints In The Sand

Of the "J.O.B."

Day in and day out
Admitting I slave to somebody else
Money for the rich while the poor stay poor

So let me ask you something . . .

When will the day come
You set yourself free
And live your life
Your destiny?

It is up to you . . .

Stay on autopilot
And keep paying the toll
Or wake up
And set a new goal!

Losing Hope

I was praying . . .

Did you not hear me?

I spoke my prayers both out loud and in silence
Waiting for miracles to be handed my way
Because I deserve them
Wanting proof that an all mighty power
Does exist and hears me

I waited for a sign . . .

I Prayed
And
I Hoped

But you did not hear me!
You were not listening!
And now my faith has been shattered

What happens when we lose hope?

The world becomes a little dimmer
We become heavier in spirit
And sadness encompasses our soul

Until the day we remember
Hope is all we have
And love is all there is

So why not, have hope?

Her

He claimed he thought her mind was beautiful
Her knowledge of love was undeniable
Her voice stirred his soul

The way she laughed gave him joy
Her eyes hypnotized him
Her lips he wanted to kiss

But these are all just words
Ones she will not miss
Because he never follows through,
their plans always a miss

When words are not enough
It's time to walk away
Life is too short . . .
for all the games that people play

Desire

My mind body and spirit are connected to you
I crave you like something sweet to eat

Sex magic, tantra, and sacred sexuality,
Ripple through my body like a strong current in a wave

Desire flows through me,
as I await my otherworldly lovers entrance

I call out your name,
a sweet, sweet, whisper in your ear

Your embrace ignites me,
energy flows freely through our touch

Together we transform,
an in-depth exploration

Where spiritual desire,
Is ignited by love and sexual pleasure

Bodies interlocked in romance,
our prophecy fulfilled

Desire

Now

She no longer plays the part

She holds memories of what once was; a broken melody
Only to be heard; in the softness of a winds gentle breeze

She no longer plays the part

She can't remember how; memories long forgotten
In the stillness of what is . . .

"Now"

Buried Alive

With each and every passing thought,
I was slowly dying . . .
Under the refuse of other people's

**OPINIONS,
PREJUDICES,
AND PREFERENCES,**

I was entombed
Expectations of society
Buried me alive

Don't Look Back

Don't look back
When you head for the door
'Cause if you do,
It'll only hurt more.

Don't stop to explain
don't tell me why.
If you're going to leave,
Just tell me good-bye.

I love you, I'll miss you
But I can make it alone.
I want you, I need you,
But I'll hold my own.

'Cause I can't tie you down,
you've got to be free.
And I can't make you
Love only me.

So don't look back,
I'll tell you again.
Just kiss me good-bye
if this is the end.

Worn

All colors fade with time;
much like memories do
Once vibrant and full of life;
until time grabs hold and washes away all the yesterdays
Leaving behind only faded memories;
and fragmented colors that have changed with time.

Upside Down

Underneath the push and pull
Polluted thoughts of rights and wrongs
Society speaking its terms aloud
Independents not a part of the crowd
Dependent on the need to provide
Education is what's keeping you alive

Darkened hopes and dreams
Oppressed by economic decline
Weakened at the seams
None the less, it's up to you how to get out of this mess

. . . Or remain upside down, in brokenness.

The Climb

Resting on the step
One day I know it's time
So I take another step.

I sit comfortably
Time passes by...
Resting easy on this step.

Feeling restless
I need to move...
So I take another step.

I see more
I feel high
So I chill on this step.

Time passes by...
I want more
So I take another step.

As I climb
I come to realize
Life is like a ladder . . .

And I must have patience.

Living in Loves Illusion

We claimed to love one another
But we were not truthful about our love
Our feelings based on sexual desires
And the meeting of our needs

We found escape in our loving moments
Filling our own, internal voids
Living in loves illusion
Something we tried so hard to avoid

Wanting to hold you close to me
To fill my desires needs
But our lack of true depth
Brings out jealousy

You break into a million pieces
Expectations left unfulfilled
When you're filled with envy
I cannot be your shield

Because I know the difference
Possessiveness and jealousy
Have no room in love
I hold you one last time

And I let you go in love.

Kissing the Rain

They sky suddenly became dark;
the devils soul present

Dark heavy clouds pregnant with malice,
suddenly unleash hypnotic sonic booms

His deep hidden anger;
sets tornados loose to roam free

Tension releases jagged bolts of lightning,
aiming specifically for me

Reality collapsing down
on my imprisoned soul

I refuse to be the victim
The devil; will not collect his toll

My tongue captures salted tears;
as I kiss the rain

My Muse is Gone

You left me in silence
No words spoken or written
Alone with thoughts
That quietly ran away,
Because they too;
had nothing to say

I want you back
I want to feel your essence
So deeply within
That I bleed ink . . .
You will be;
the adulation of my pen

Break Through

Break Through
Clouds rapidly in motion
Floating through the sky
Until a break through occurred
And the light kissed the land
Shining the light of hope
Glorified and grand

The beauty of Gods working hands

Thorns

Our blood lineage is so inextricably connected;
It's like a rose to the thorn.
Beautiful to admire;
But defensive if touched the wrong way.

Self-Image

I stepped outside of myself
And took a look at me
I really must admit,
I don't like what I see

I am not myself
Nor who I want to be
I have become the image
of a judgmental society

My thighs are too big
My stomach isn't flat
I must be ugly
Cause I really am fat

I look at myself in the mirror
And am disgusted with what I see
Visualizing the fat girl
That is dying to be free

Adolescence Eating Disorder Statistics:

> ➢ *Anorexia is the third most common chronic illness among adolescents*
>
> ➢ *95% of those who have eating disorders are between the ages of 12 and 25*

Statistics by: National Association of Anorexia Nervosa and Associated Disorders

Rise of the Holes

When you left, I dug a hole. Digging deep into the layers of my emptiness. I lost my value, loss my love, loss my strength, loss my clarity, and all of my essence.

The deeper I dug the more I realized I allowed you to fill my holes. Unconsciously I did not see that part of you makes me feel my value as separate from me; I see it as part of you filling my holes with hope and destiny.

I felt "we fit each other" feeling fully complete, a unified whole, one that could sustain the dissatisfaction of us being incomplete. I filled you, and you filled me, together creating our own sustainability.

And now my holes are caving and shaking with fear knowing you are no longer here. I feel the emptiness and I take stride, the memory of what was lost, and knowing my essence will start to rise.

Through it all I have learned…. It is not in the filling of my holes, but in the "feeling" of understanding the power that creates the holes that fills me up with the essence of loving the life I live once again, allowing the holes to subside never to feel separate from self again.

Walking In

Wondering

I wondered if things would be different
If a shift in our current environments
Can bring the changes we both desire?

Would it be worth taking a chance?
Letting vulnerability lay on the table
Having to rely on faith in choices made

I wonder how we will approach this
Will we be apprehensive?
And maybe, stray away . . .

Or . . . will we just dive right in
Like a perfect fit
In a universal design?

Wondering

Unconditionally

Your kids don't care what you are wearing
Or what you buy them
Or what schools they get into
They just want you there,
That's it.

Time is running out . . .

They won't love you unconditionally that much longer
So for your own good
Don't miss out
On really getting to know them

They are truly amazing little people!

Our children;
Our greatest privilege.

Forgotten

I am a shadow of my former self;
A ghost,
a memory long forgotten,
one that was hidden and left to die.

Some Day

I imagine . . .
Someday I will find myself

The self that has been waiting for me all along

I will stop stumbling about in the dark,
Fearing the unknown,
and withdrawing from the world

One day I will awaken,
And be like . . .

"Hey, there you are!"

You will take me by the hand and lead me to the light

We will greet each other
and our hearts will know,
Our journey has just begun . . .

I found myself today,
I am the unity of one.

Broken Compass

Feeling incomplete
I realize I lost myself
Completely unaware of where I went
To busy in the hustle of life
I guess?
Outweighed by the
Necessity to provide
Always following the standards
Living as you expect me to.

…Trapped in roles such as Mom, Spouse, Employee, and things we do.

Suddenly awakened to another level of
Existence
Living a life in tune with my authentic self means
Finding my skills, talents, and wisdom.

… Because relying on information from the fictional self is like trusting a broken compass.

Finger Jams

I am the cord

that you strum

The vibration of sound

created by your finger tip

The callus,

holds the memory of every note

Sweeping delightfully

along my cord

Together we make music beautifully

I Found the Hidden Self

The endless stories of the past
Follow me through life
Flashing visions of the hidden self

Separate from life in this moment
I am lost in the illusion of today
Longing to feel connected in some way

Ten thousand worries preoccupy my mind
The world
Life
My family
And the day-to-day grind

But can't you see... An occupied mind can't be free?

As quickly as you let it
Your mind makes a movie
Showing the possibilities
The Future and the Past

Your mind presenting pictures
And making up the story
Based on your perception
And the feelings of that time

I want to be free from the past!

How am I to hear the songs of the birds?
And the sound of the breeze,
With a mind constantly preoccupied?

Imprints In The Sand

By taking the vow to live in the now
Breaking the habit of an auto-tuned mind
Letting go of the need to always define

My mind no longer needing to…

Explain it
Know it
Compare it
And store it
Time after time

I finally freed myself and my mind stays right here and lives in the now!

Respectfully Aging

My face reflects my regrets, stresses and troubles
Each and every line, wrinkle and crevice . . .

Years of struggling to survive,
now shown to the world
like a map of my life in full view

Time ravaging my body
my time here; half spent
What in the world will I do?

Remember my purpose,
enjoy the journey,
and look at myself; anew

Imprints In The Sand

Now Here

Broken Heart

This pain inside me . . .

Rips me,
Tears me,
And breaks me down
It's turned my life upside down

Ripped,
Torn,
And broken

I wade through the depths of my broken heart . . .

I am reminded that once in awhile
Life seems to turn you upside down
So you can remember . . .
How to live right side up again

Releasing the pain within in this tender heart . . .

Claiming I am ready,
To heal and move on
Forever a memory held in the heart
Forgiveness the first place, I will start.

Time Keeps on Slipping Into the Future

I have come to realize
That before me lies blank pages
Ready for me to pen . .

No matter what has happened in the past
With the breaking dawn of each new day
My future is always ready to be written

My tomorrows filled with all my dreams
Waiting to be created
Waiting to arrive at the scripted scene

At any moment I am able to be whom I dream to be
To create my future
And my destiny

So with this pen in hand
And blank pages too
I re-create this story

This very minute I make a choice . . .

And decide how it will unfold
Changing the central characters
And creating a new ending

Because this we know . . .

Time keeps on slipping into the future
And it's never too late to become
The person you have always wanted to be.

I Am Love

I am the Wind beneath your wings
Empowering your stance

I am the Warmth of the sunset
Shining upon your skin

I am the Quietness
You hear when you are alone

I am the Feeling
Of Butterflies in your stomach fluttering around

I am the Light
That shines love and happiness for everyone to see

I am the Strength
That holds you upright

I am the Love
That encompasses all

I AM … The Love I am destined to be.

The Reach

I extend my hand to you
Hoping for the right fit
As you fingers slide between mine
In the holding hand commitment

We hold each other's hands
As we walk down the street
Smiles on our faces
Interlocked finger embraces

Loving this feeling
Of holding on to you
You make me feel so happy
In simply being you

Hoping to hold your hand
Each and every day
I wonder if you are the one
That will steal my heart away?

And so I let down these walls
And I offer you my hand
Giving you my heart…
While reaching for your hand.

Soul House

Barefooted she walks,
carrying the weight of the world in her womb

Striped of her impurities,
each and every step she took

She walked the beating path of indiscretion,
her heart is racing with each and every step

Her self-worth gave way to the wind long ago,
She pushes forward to forget

Step after step,
burying the past; with each foot forward

Fighting her own inner demons
on her journey along the way

Until that which is dark,
becomes light

Belief in self,
washes away the broken tears

She is awakened,
and now understands . .

Beneath the roof of her soul
Love Enlightens

Spiritual Fool

Realizations begin to set in
Anger is ranting within me
I have not met my own expectations
I am mad I allow so many distractions in my life
I create busyness as a coping mechanism
I am disappointed that I feel dispirited
I have become inattentive to love

Spiritual Fool . . .

Why are you wasting so much time being in your head;
instead of in your life?

My Wish For You

With each in breath I imagine our compassion growing, like a glowing ember being blown upon so that its brightness and intensity steadily increases.

Inhale…. I think "May you be free from suffering." May I take all of your suffering and negativity upon myself right now.

With each out breath, I imagine our love growing, again like a glowing ember growing in brightness and intensity.

Exhale…. I think "May you be happy. May you find true and lasting happiness. May you find inner peace."

With each round of breath my visualization and intention Is so strong in faith, I AM creating the causes for these wishes to be accomplished.

Wishing you peace and happiness.

Path to Dharma

Peacefully I walk
Aligning with spirit
Transforming my mind to a natural state
Heading into uncharted open-heart space

Temporary conditions dissolved
Once we open our eyes, minds and hearts

Discovering we are our own source of our difficulties
Hence the reason to look within
And enter deeply into the present
Remembering our relatedness
Manifesting a (k)new reality
And finding truth in one's heart

Acting in concert with ones divine purpose in life.

Observation

I desperately wanted to yell out to you
But you walked away, and shut the door
It was like a horrible dream where I had no voice
I could only watch your actions play out in front of me

My desire to be an observer of life
Is actually keeping me from living one.

Incomplete

I need you
With all your jagged edges
Rounded corners
And smooth surfaces

Without you
I am half a story
Waiting to be finished
Incomplete

You are the missing piece.

Katana

Gentle rhythms
Silence the night
Cut by the blade of the sword

In one single swooping action
Everything cuts way to the NOW
A captured moment of freedom

Inevitable death
Performed daily in trance
Is the substance to the way of the samurai

10,000 arrows will not rip me apart
Nor will rifles,
Spears or swords

May I be carried away by surging waves
Thrown into the midst of a raging fire
Or struck by lightning from the Gods above

But to bring death upon a master . . .

I will die 10,000 deaths
Consider me dead
My soul becomes one with the sword

Broken Mirrors

Shards of glass hold fragmented images
While unclaimed darkness lurking in the shadows
Waits to cast judgments upon our rejected and disowned image

False projections cast reflections of unworthiness
Disclaiming our own greatness
With fear and self-doubt

Unconsciously looking in the mirror daily
Projecting ugliness with one's own thoughts
Dislikes running wild in a rampart playground of false ideas and beliefs

"I am not good enough"
Running truth in your ears
The projections of only, your deepest fears

Uncomfortable with the sight that is magnified and seen
Not a picture cut out of a beauty magazine
Righteously upset with the hand you were dealt

Angry,
Hypocritical
Nasty, the emotions you felt

Blaming the broken mirror for the image it casts
Close minded descriptions of your focal view
Your own self-image dissected right in front of you.

Shadow Effect

Judgmental minds follow me
Scratching only at the outer surface of who I am
My own thoughts creating shadows in the light

Selflessly projecting what I want you to see
The question is . . .
Do you know the real me?

Hidden behind a pretty face
Thoughts on lock down
Creating a superficial mind space

Allowing fear to hold me back
Personalities dip into an empty abyss
Creating life altering destructiveness

The dark side exists
It's always right there
It begins the moment you sense fear

When we embrace all of who we are
The good, bad, light and dark
We can become the flame, and light the spark

It is our birthright to have it all

Imprints In The Sand

So do not allow the shadow to cast its spell
And keep you in a living hell

Take the journey back to love
Voiding the shadow with the releasing of fears
The dualistic self is now, right here

With an honest look we will see ourselves
Stepping beyond perception into our authentic self
Reconnecting the person we are meant to be

The Question is, will you know the real me?

The Machine

With closed eyes we walk straight lines
Forgetting to open our eyes and dance in the intersections
We have become a living machine

Wandering through life looking for the connection
Missing opportunities because of lack of perception
We are driven by technology and its misconception

Forgetting to stop and connect all the dots
The machine took over
And has created the plot

Not able to bend and see the light
Lost in the illusion of the day-to-day grind
Being driven . . . by a one track mind

Break the shackles
And set yourself free
We are one-of-a-kind species, we are humanity

Connect with people
And create the space
Death of the machine we will celebrate

Because you and I, we are one
We dance in the intersections

Imprints In The Sand

The exchange just begun . . .

So step out of the machine
And take my hand
Together we will walk re-creating the plot

Time is relevant
Let's walk in the now
Death to the machine, that is how.

Landscapes

Watching the beauty of days end, fade into darkness
Roses bending with the blackened weight of your absence
I hold you in my heart, and carry you in my presence
I am willing to travel, in time and distance

Bleak landscapes define our separation
Sunrises and sunsets we watch alone
We go to the truth beyond the mind
Where love is the bridge we try to define

The union of love
Knows no extremes of distance
In the mind ever burning
We let go of resistance

Traveling desert landscapes and mountains high
Lapping waves bring me ashore
The longing I feel for you
I will feel no more

All of Me

Love not the divine essence of just my petals
Captured alone in the heart,
They become wilted and decay

Love all of me;
Then you will love the essence of my petals
The thorns along my spine,
The emerging bud opening
The dance of divine

Loving life in its fullness
It knows no decay
Living in the present
of this special day

The scent of full love
Has set itself free
Knowing no boundaries
Loving all of me

Ebb and Flow

The stillness of your presence
Washes over me like a soft lapping wave
The give and take of the tide pushing inward
Gently gravitates me toward

The sound of your voice
A soft echoing whisper
Vibrating in the darkened night
My ear can't help but to lean in

And at last . . .

You touch me
With a soft caressing sensation
That awakens my soul
And lifts my spirit higher

In that moment . . .

We experienced the truth of our ebb and flow.

Amplified Love

My soul knows the truth . . .

Love is everywhere I look
In every person
And every situation

Amplified love will
Wake even the buried
Absent and hidden

Difficult situations contain the seeds of love
They are waiting to emerge
To awaken the dormant heart

Dead layers peeling off and shedding
Awoken by the beating heart
Beat by beat love begins to emanate once again

Let your soul amplify
And light up the love that lies within you
Like the brightest star in the sky

Acknowledge all the love
Compassion and kindness
You already express and embody

Feel the soul love flowing within you
Let the divine light pour out of you
And the seeds planted will grow

Amplify love, and you will increase it.

When I see you

When I gaze upon you
I notice your little neck
Your thinning hair
Your crooked teeth
Your blemished skin
Your breasts that no longer stand
Your abundant stomach
Your big hips
Your thick thighs

And in that moment . . .

I see myself

Some days
I tilt my neck to the right
I whisk my sexy hair
I smile back
I embrace my skin
I love my breasts
I cherish the womb that bore children
I sway my hips
And my thighs ground me

A beautiful woman . . .

I see myself

Understanding Emptiness

Piece by piece I built the wall
Isolating myself from the world
Trapped in loneliness

Behind the wall I felt secure
Protected from the ravages of life
And lack of relationships

But then one day I am awakened
Coming to the understanding that to be lonely
Is to not have a true relationship with life

The lack of relationship with life is the emptiness
That caused the despair and loneliness
And created my separateness

As long as the wall exists
I cannot banish my emptiness
Or escape the loneliness

So piece by piece
I tear you down
And boldly enter the heart of emptiness

Understanding that the emptiness was
The absence of love
And that love can only flow when the wall is demolished

I am breaking down the wall of emptiness.

Without Notice

Spirit whispered softly in my ear
Prompting me to make a move
The question is,
do I listen?

An intuitive mind reaching out to mine
Looking to make connection
The question is,
do I pay attention?

Without Notice
I take action
And show up at your door.

Divorce: Losing What You Know

When one become two
No burdens left undone
The children are still "ours"
In parenting 101

You can walk away . . .
And claim a new life for yourself
But don't forget the kids
This is what our life is all about

We laid down and made a baby
That was the easy part to do
But when it comes to parenting
Will you be there and come through?

The choice is really yours
I can't make you feel . . .
That your child is important
And is counting on you still

Support to be paid
It was a court order
Just because you pay it
It doesn't make you a father

So within this journey

Imprints In The Sand

And this hand I was dealt
I turned "two" back into "one"

Finding Mother and Father in myself

It really is too bad
You are completely missing out
I raised the greatest children
Our love stretches out . . .

Parenting 101, I work on by myself.

Summer Rain

The storm is coming . .

You can hear the thunder getting closer
The smell of rain is in the air

I stood on my balcony
and breathed deeply
While the wind blew
softly through and against me

I thought to myself . . . "She's Coming"

I can smell her in the distance
I close my eyes and wait,
wait for the rain

Oh how I love,
Love the summer rain

HELLO SUN, Goodbye Moon
(A Mother and Son Collaboration)

The sun rose from the other side of the earth
Waking us to a bright new day
We are joyful that the darkness has gone
And that the sun returned shining it's beautiful rays

Sitting in the clouds up high
Smiling with its pretty blues eyes
The color of the oceans deep
The shining star is not asleep

As I stand under the sun feeling hopeful and cheerful
Enjoying this hot summers day
The sun shines its beautiful rays upon this earth
For all to enjoy its intense bright beauty

The sun is there to guide this day
Warming my skin as I play
And when it's time to say good night
I patiently wait, knowing the sun goes to visit the other side of the earth

And so I go to bed waiting to wake up and say HELLO SUN.

Isiah Williams, Age 11

The moon sits in a silent darkened sky
Lit up stars near and far his only friends
Everyone is sleeping in his presence

Imprints In The Sand

I wonder does the moon become jealous of the sun?

Since everyone is awake and ready to play
The sun stealing the show, of every single day

Or does the moon simply send us to bed?
Providing us with dreams that dance in our heads
Giving us hours of rest as we lay up in our beds

Dreaming of tomorrows plays in the sun
I can't wait to go out to play and run
I wish the sun would hurry on back

So I can say, "Goodbye Moon, the Sun is Back!"

Raja Williams

> I was working on my manuscript *The Journey Along The Way* when my son Isiah came into my room and decided he wanted to write too. He asked "could he write with me?" So I said "let's do a timed writing to a picture." We choose a picture from the internet and both sat down for 15 minutes and wrote whatever the picture inspired. Isiah had a full page, and I had three stanzas. Together Isiah and I picked out lines from his page of writing to form his stanzas. He was excited, he never wrote a poem before. As you can see, he focused on details, while I spent more time on form. This is our original, I would love to edit mine. But none the less, it was a great writing exercise with my son. Bravo Isiah, may your observations of life always be expressed creatively. Love you, Mom.

Personal Fiction

We are paying a high price for our unawareness
Believing that our ideas and opinions; are truth
Yet, they are mere thoughts of a human

Preoccupation with a past that has already occurred,
or with a future that hasn't arrived yet
Paying the toll; for willful ignoring of the present moment

The fallout accumulates silently;
Coloring our lives without notice
Fictional thoughts; replacing the truth of the moment

Our personal fiction steps in....

We believe we already know who we are,
We know where we are, and where were going,
We know what's happening . . .

All the while we are enshrouded in . . .

THOUGHTS,
FANTASIES,
AND IMPULSES

Our thoughts are in the past,
Our thoughts are in the future,
Our thoughts are dissecting what we want and what we like

Our mind is spinning continuously . . .

Imprints In The Sand

Revealing our direction and the very ground we stand upon
I let go of my personal fiction; I choose to be in the now
Living in this moment, creating right now.

Q & A's with Myself

There comes a time in one's life
No matter the age, young or old
Or somewhere in between
When we have questions …

And we expect answers!

I sit down and think to myself
All the things I ponder
And I can't help but wonder
Am I following my lives path?

The questions I must ask myself:

Question: What is happiness to you?

Answer: A feeling that comes from within.
Each individual feels and experiences
happiness in different levels. You are
responsible for your own happiness.
You cannot rely on someone else to
make you feel happy.

Question: Are you content?

Answer: No, I am always feeling the
need to move and expand.
I dislike stagnate periods of time
that make you feel trapped in the
day to day habits of life.

Question: What is love to you?

Imprints In The Sand

Answer: Love is a deep emotion that we
experience and feel. There are many
different kinds of love. For example
the union of two lovers. A mothers
love for her children. Love for a pet, your
friends and neighbors, as well as others
you connect with. The most important
thing about love is that it should always
be an unconditional offering. Just because I
love you, doesn't mean you have to love me
the same way. Just love!

Question: Are you doing what you want to do?

Answer: At times, I am able to fulfill my wants
and desires. Some of them are things that will
require time to obtain. With that being said I
am gainfully employed at a job that fulfills my
financial needs and suffices daily living. I have
set goals and utilize creative energy which drives
my passion and fuels my world. So, yes.

Question: Are you living in the now?

Answer: Although I have learned enough
about life to know and understand that to
be in the now, is a wonderful gift, but not
as easily obtained as one would think. To be
in the now means: I am completely present
in this moment. There are no past memories
attached. I am not visualizing or thinking

about possible futures either. It means I am living
in this moment right here, right now, as it is.

* I slip in and out, but I am grounded in the "Now" more
often then not.

Question: Are you on the right path?

Answer: An individual's path is a sacred journey
initially guided by ones upbringing. You at some
point gain self-control and have the free will to
follow your own path. The journey has many
twists and turns throughout the years,
making it easy for ones path to alter.
Simply follow your guidance and be true
to ones self and the path shall always
be clear to you.

* End Q & A

Yes I sat and spoke with myself
Had a conversation
Connected with my higher self
As strange as this may be . . .

I quickly came to see the benefits
of connecting mentally
I answered my own questions
And clearly you must see …

I walk this path with good intention, connecting in Love &
Spiritually.

Epilogue

"Together let's unleash our creative talents and share them with the world!"

– Raja's Insight

About the Author

Ms. Raja Williams, also known as Raja's Insight, fiercely arrived on the writer's scene in 2012 after being awakened by a prolific poet, lyricist, songwriter, and music producer whom encouraged her to write daily. After nearly twenty years of pent up words only floating in her own head she began to allow the words to spill out onto empty pages and find way to readers needing encouraging words. Raja entered one of her poems into a poetry contest in 2013 and won a full publishing contract and released her first book "*The Journey Along The Way*" in January of 2014 with Inner Child Press.

Through the publishing process and having connected with so many amazing writers and poets from around the world Raja was moved to create a community for writers known as

"Creative Talents Unleashed."

Having spent her entire working career in teaching and mentoring positions Raja found herself mentoring writers and walking them through the entire publishing process. Soon Creative Talents Unleashed moved from a writer's community to a publishing group. Within the publishing group Raja founded a program called the "Starving Artist Fund" to assist writers in having the necessary tools to become published authors at little to no financial cost.

Raja is living her life's purpose, and enjoys assisting writers from all around the world give birth and share their creative talents with the world through publishing.

Raja's Links

Facebook

www.facebook.com/RajasInsight
www.facebook.com/CreativeTalentsUnleashed

Blog

www.RajasInsight.com

Twitter

@Rajasinsight

Instagram

https://instagram.com/rajasinsight/

Soundcloud

https://soundcloud.com/rajas-insight

Author Page

www.ctupublishinggroup.com/raja-williams-.html

www.ctupublishinggroup.com

Creative Talents Unleashed is an independent publishing group that offers writers an opportunity to share their writing talents with the world. We are committed to fostering and honoring the work of writers of all cultures.

For More Information Contact:

info@ctupublishinggroup.com

www.ingramcontent.com/pod-product-compliance
Lightning Source LLC
Chambersburg PA
CBHW071313060426
42444CB00034B/2040